To:

....

From:

....

Date:

....

PEACE *in* HIS PRESENCE

FAVORITE QUOTATIONS FROM **Jesus Calling**®

Sarah Young

THOMAS NELSON
Since 1798

Peace in His Presence: Favorite Quotations from Jesus Calling®

© 2015 by Sarah Young

Published in Nashville, Tennessee, by Thomas Nelson. Thomas Nelson is a registered trademark of HarperCollins Christian Publishing, Inc.

Photographs are from Shutterstock.com.

Thomas Nelson titles may be purchased in bulk for educational, business, fund-raising, or sales promotional use. For information, please e-mail SpecialMarkets@ThomasNelson.com.

Unless otherwise noted, Scripture quotations are taken from the Holy Bible, New International Version®, NIV®. Copyright © 1973, 1978, 1984 by Biblica, Inc.™ Used by permission of Zondervan. All rights reserved worldwide. www.zondervan.com.

Scripture quotations marked AMP are taken from THE AMPLIFIED BIBLE: OLD TESTAMENT. ©1962, 1964 by Zondervan (used by permission); and from THE AMPLIFIED BIBLE: NEW TESTAMENT. © 1958 by the Lockman Foundation (used by permission). Scripture quotations marked NASB are taken from NEW AMERICAN STANDARD BIBLE®. © The Lockman Foundation 1960, 1962, 1963, 1968, 1971, 1972, 1973, 1975, 1977. Used by permission. Scripture quotations marked NKJV are taken from THE NEW KING JAMES VERSION. © 1982 by Thomas Nelson, Inc. Used by permission. All rights reserved. Scripture quotations marked ESV are from the ENGLISH STANDARD VERSION. © 2001 by Crossway Bibles, a division of Good News Publishers.

ISBN-13: 978-0-7180-3416-0

Printed in China

18 19 20 DSC 7 6 5 4

Dear Reader,

As you peruse the pages of this book, I hope you will enjoy the beauty of God's glorious creation and find comfort in Jesus' Peace.

The quotations taken from *Jesus Calling* are written from the perspective of Jesus speaking to *you*, the reader. I have included Scripture with each of the quotations, and I encourage you to read *both*—slowly and thoughtfully.

I will be praying for readers of *Peace in His Presence*. I consider this a joyful privilege and a delightful responsibility.

Bountiful blessings!

Sarah Young

Now may the Lord of peace himself give you
peace at all times and in every way.

—2 Thessalonians 3:16

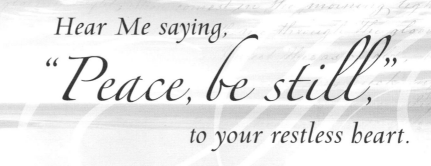

Hear Me saying,
"*Peace, be still,*"
to your restless heart.

Then He arose and rebuked the wind, and
said to the sea, "Peace, be still!" And the wind
ceased and there was a great calm.

—MARK 4:39 NKJV

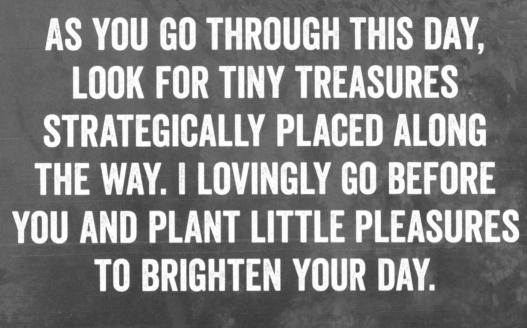

AS YOU GO THROUGH THIS DAY, LOOK FOR TINY TREASURES STRATEGICALLY PLACED ALONG THE WAY. I LOVINGLY GO BEFORE YOU AND PLANT LITTLE PLEASURES TO BRIGHTEN YOUR DAY.

THOSE WHO LOOK TO HIM ARE RADIANT; THEIR FACES ARE NEVER COVERED WITH SHAME.

—Psalm 34:5

DO NOT FEAR YOUR
WEAKNESS, FOR IT IS
THE STAGE ON WHICH
MY POWER AND MY
GLORY PERFORM
MOST BRILLIANTLY.

Let all who take refuge in you be glad;
Let them ever sing for joy.

—*PSALM 5:11*

I am the firm Foundation

on which you can *dance*

and *sing* and celebrate **My** **P**resence.

"I will never leave you nor forsake you."

—Joshua 1:5

MY POWER FLOWS MOST FREELY INTO WEAK ONES AWARE OF THEIR NEED FOR ME. FALTERING STEPS OF DEPENDENCE ARE NOT LACK OF FAITH; THEY ARE LINKS TO MY PRESENCE.

He gives strength to the weary and increases the power of the weak. . . . They will soar on wings like eagles; they will run and not grow weary, they will walk and not be faint.

—ISAIAH 40:29, 31

Nothing is *wasted* when it is shared with Me.

I can bring beauty out of the ashes of lost *dreams*.

I can glean *Joy* out of sorrow, *Peace* out of adversity.

Only a Friend who is also the *King* of kings

could accomplish this divine alchemy.

Sorrowful, yet always rejoicing; poor, yet making many rich;
having nothing, and yet possessing everything.

—2 CORINTHIANS 6:10

Accept each day just as it comes to you.
Do not waste your time and energy wishing for a
different set of circumstances. Instead, *trust*
Me enough to yield to My design and purposes.

The LORD gives strength to his people;
the LORD blesses his people with peace.
—PSALM 29:11

Miracles ARE NOT ALWAYS VISIBLE TO THE NAKED EYE, BUT THOSE WHO LIVE BY *faith* CAN SEE THEM CLEARLY. LIVING BY FAITH, RATHER THAN SIGHT, ENABLES YOU TO SEE MY *glory*.

We live by faith, not by sight.

—2 CORINTHIANS 5:7

If you learn to *trust* Me—really trust Me—with your whole being, then nothing can separate you from My Peace. Everything you *endure* can be put to good use by allowing it to train you in trusting Me. This is how you foil the works of evil, growing in *grace* through the very adversity that was meant to harm you.

Trust in the LORD forever, for the LORD, the LORD, is the Rock eternal.

—ISAIAH 26:4

Remember that there is no condemnation for

those who belong to Me. You have been

judged NOT GUILTY *for all eternity.*

Trust Me, and don't be afraid;

for I am your Strength, Song, and Salvation.

Therefore, there is now no condemnation for those who are in Christ Jesus, because through Christ Jesus the law of the Spirit of life set me free from the law of sin and death.

–ROMANS 8:1-2

Gently bring your attention
back to Me, whenever it wanders away.
I look for persistence—rather
than perfection—in your
walk with Me.

I am like an olive tree flourishing in the house of God;
I trust in God's unfailing love for ever and ever.

—Psalm 52:8

TO RECEIVE MY *Peace*, YOU MUST CHANGE YOUR GRASPING, CONTROLLING STANCE TO ONE OF OPENNESS AND TRUST. THE ONLY THING YOU CAN GRASP WITHOUT DAMAGING YOUR SOUL IS MY HAND.

God is our refuge and strength,
an ever-present help in trouble.

—PSALM 46:1

By GAZING at Me, you gain My PERSPECTIVE on your life. This time alone with Me is ESSENTIAL for unscrambling your THOUGHTS and smoothing out the day before you.

Within your temple, *O God,* we meditate on your unfailing love.

—PSALM 48:9

"Indeed, the very hairs of your head are all numbered. Don't be afraid; you are worth more than many sparrows."

—*Luke 12:7*

I, the *Lover* of your *soul*, understand you *perfectly* and love you eternally.

EACH MOMENT YOU CAN CHOOSE TO PRACTICE MY PRESENCE OR TO PRACTICE THE PRESENCE OF PROBLEMS.

"I have come as a **LIGHT** into the world, that whoever believes in Me should not abide in darkness."

—John 12:46 NKJV

But since we belong to the day, let us be self-controlled, putting on faith and love as a breastplate, and the hope of salvation as a helmet.

–1 Thessalonians 5:8

I AM TRAINING YOU to HOLD in YOUR HEART a DUAL FOCUS: MY CONTINUAL PRESENCE and the HOPE of HEAVEN.

Though I may *lead* you along *paths* that feel alien to you, trust that I know what I am doing. If you *follow* Me wholeheartedly, you will discover *facets* of yourself that were previously hidden.

"WHAT GOOD IS IT FOR A MAN TO GAIN THE WHOLE WORLD, YET FORFEIT HIS SOUL?"

—*Mark 8:36*

Every time you thank Me, you acknowledge that I am your Lord and Provider. This is the proper stance for a child of God: receiving with thanksgiving.

LET THEM GIVE *thanks* TO THE LORD FOR HIS UNFAILING LOVE AND HIS WONDERFUL DEEDS FOR MEN. LET THEM SACRIFICE THANK OFFERINGS AND TELL OF HIS WORKS WITH SONGS OF JOY.

—*Psalm 107:21-22*

Receive **My Peace** as
you lie down to sleep, with
thankful thoughts playing a
lullaby in your mind.

I will lie down and sleep in peace, for you alone,

O Lord, make me dwell in safety.

—*Psalm 4:8*

A *successful* DAY IS
ONE IN WHICH YOU HAVE STAYED
IN TOUCH WITH ME, EVEN IF
MANY THINGS REMAIN UNDONE
AT THE END OF THE DAY.

Pray continually.

—1 THESSALONIANS 5:17

INSTEAD OF STRIVING FOR A PREDICTABLE, SAFE LIFESTYLE, SEEK TO KNOW ME IN GREATER DEPTH AND BREADTH. I WANT TO MAKE YOUR LIFE A GLORIOUS ADVENTURE, BUT YOU MUST STOP CLINGING TO OLD WAYS.

When I am afraid, I will trust in you. In God, whose word I praise, in God I trust; I will not be afraid. What can mortal man do to me?

—PSALM 56:3–4

My kingdom is not about earning and deserving; it is about believing and receiving.

"So I say to you: Ask and it will be given to you; seek and you will find; knock and the door will be opened to you. For everyone who asks receives; he who seeks finds; and to him who knocks, the door will be opened."

—Luke 11:9–10

Whenever you are *tempted* to grumble,

come to Me and talk it out. As you open up to Me,

I will put My *song* in your *heart*.

Do everything without complaining or arguing,
so that you may become blameless and pure,
children of God without fault in a crooked
and depraved generation, in which you shine
like stars in the universe.

—*Philippians 2:14–15*

My grace is sufficient for you,

but its sufficiency is for one day at a time.

"Therefore do not worry
about tomorrow, for tomorrow
will worry about itself. Each day
has enough trouble of its own."

— Matthew 6:34

GUARD YOUR THOUGHTS DILIGENTLY. GOOD THOUGHT-CHOICES WILL KEEP YOU CLOSE TO ME.

Search me, O God, and know my heart; try me and know my anxious thoughts; and see if there be any hurtful way in me, and lead me in the everlasting way.

—PSALM 139:23–24 NASB

Consider it pure joy, my brothers, whenever you face trials of many kinds, because you know that the testing of your faith develops perseverance.

—James 1:2–3

Thank Me when things do not go your way, because *spiritual blessings* come wrapped in trials.

I long for you to **trust** *Me enough to be fully yourself with Me. When you are* **real** *with Me, I am able to bring out the best in you: the very gifts I have* **planted** *in your soul.*

"Greater love has no one than this, that he lay down his life for his friends. You are my friends if you do what I command. . . . I have called you friends, for everything that I learned from my Father I have made known to you."

—*John 15:13–15*

This is the day that I have made! As you rejoice in this day of life, it will yield up to you precious gifts and beneficial training.

You are my God, and I will give you thanks; you are my God, and I will exalt you.

—Psalm 118:28

I AM ALWAYS BEFORE YOU, BECKONING YOU ON—ONE STEP AT A TIME. NEITHER HEIGHT NOR DEPTH, NOR ANYTHING ELSE IN ALL CREATION, CAN SEPARATE YOU FROM MY LOVING PRESENCE.

For I am convinced that neither death nor life, neither angels nor demons, neither the present nor the future, nor any powers, neither height nor depth, nor anything else in all creation, will be able to separate us from the love of God that is in Christ Jesus our Lord.

—*Romans 8:38–39*

Invite Me into your thoughts by whispering
My Name. Suddenly your day brightens.

In the morning, O Lord, you hear my voice; in the morning I lay my requests before you and wait in expectation.

—Psalm 5:3

Marvel at the wonder of being able to commune with the King of the universe—any time, any place. Never take this amazing privilege for granted!

"For my thoughts are not your thoughts, neither are your ways my ways," declares the LORD. "As the heavens are higher than the earth, so are my ways higher than your ways and my thoughts than your thoughts."

—ISAIAH 55:8–9

THANK ME FOR
THE GIFT OF MY PEACE:
A GIFT OF SUCH IMMENSE
PROPORTIONS THAT YOU
CANNOT FATHOM ITS
DEPTH OR BREADTH.

~~~

Let the peace of Christ rule in your hearts,
since as members of one body you were
called to peace. And be thankful.

—*Colossians 3:15*

You will always face trouble in this life. But more importantly, you will always have Me with you, helping you handle whatever you encounter. Approach problems with a light touch by viewing them in My *revealing* Light.

"I have told you these things, so that in me you may have peace. In this world you will have trouble. But take heart! I have overcome the world."

—JOHN 16:33

ALTHOUGH SELF-SUFFICIENCY IS ACCLAIMED IN THE WORLD, RELIANCE ON ME PRODUCES ABUNDANT LIVING IN MY KINGDOM.

"I am the vine; you are the branches.
If a man remains in me and I in him, he will bear much fruit;
apart from me you can do nothing."

—JOHN 15:5

I COMPREHEND YOU IN

ALL YOUR COMPLEXITY;

NO DETAIL OF YOUR LIFE

IS HIDDEN FROM ME.

I VIEW YOU THROUGH EYES OF *grace*,

SO DON'T BE AFRAID OF

MY INTIMATE AWARENESS.

"NO ONE WILL BE ABLE TO STAND UP
AGAINST YOU ALL THE DAYS OF YOUR
LIFE. AS I WAS WITH MOSES, SO I WILL BE
WITH YOU; I WILL NEVER LEAVE YOU NOR
FORSAKE YOU."

—JOSHUA 1:5

As you live in close contact with Me,

the Light of My Presence filters through you

to *bless* others. Your weakness and woundedness

are openings through which the Light of the

knowledge of My Glory *shines* forth.

But He said to me . . . My strength and power are made perfect (fulfilled and completed) and show themselves most effective in [your] weakness.

—2 Corinthians 12:9 AMP

Remember that I can **fit** everything into a **pattern** for good, including the things you wish were different. Start with where you are at this point in time and space, **accepting** that this is where I intend you to be.

....

We are assured and know that . . . all things work together and are [fitting into a plan] for good . . . for those who love God and are called according to [His] design and purpose.

—Romans 8:28 AMP

Rather than planning and evaluating, practice

TRUSTING and THANKING Me

continually. This is a paradigm shift that will

revolutionize your life.

NOW THANKS BE TO GOD WHO ALWAYS LEADS US IN
TRIUMPH IN CHRIST, AND THROUGH US DIFFUSES THE
FRAGRANCE OF HIS KNOWLEDGE IN EVERY PLACE.

—2 CORINTHIANS 2:14 NKJV

Be willing to follow wherever I lead. I am the Light from on high that dawns upon you, to guide your feet into the way of Peace.

The Word became flesh and made his dwelling among us. We have seen his glory, the glory of the One and Only, who came from the Father, full of grace and truth.

—JOHN 1:14

WHAT I SEARCH FOR IN MY CHILDREN IS AN AWAKENED SOUL THAT THRILLS TO THE JOY OF MY PRESENCE! I CREATED MANKIND TO GLORIFY AND ENJOY ME FOREVER. I PROVIDE THE JOY; YOUR PART IS TO GLORIFY ME BY LIVING CLOSE TO ME.

I WILL *praise* YOU, O LORD MY GOD, WITH ALL MY *heart*, AND I WILL *glorify* YOUR NAME FOREVERMORE.

—PSALM 86:12 NKJV

THE INTIMACY I OFFER
YOU IS NOT AN INVITATION
TO ACT AS IF YOU WERE MY
EQUAL. WORSHIP ME AS KING
OF KINGS WHILE WALKING
HAND IN HAND WITH ME
DOWN THE PATH OF LIFE.

"Now this is eternal life: that they may know you,
the only true God, and Jesus Christ, whom you have sent."

-John 17:3

INSTEAD OF
SINGLE-MINDEDLY PURSUING
A GOAL, TALK WITH ME ABOUT IT.
LET THE LIGHT OF MY PRESENCE
SHINE ON THIS PURSUIT, SO YOU CAN
SEE IT FROM MY PERSPECTIVE.

Look to the LORD and his strength; seek his face always.

—1 Chronicles 16:11

I AM NOT A CARELESS GOD.
WHEN I ALLOW DIFFICULTIES TO
COME INTO YOUR LIFE, I EQUIP
YOU FULLY TO HANDLE THEM.

"For *nothing* is *impossible* with God."
—Luke 1:37

Spend time with Me for the pure pleasure of being in My company. I can brighten up the dullest of gray days; I can add sparkle to the routines of daily life.

BECAUSE YOU ARE MY HELP,
I SING IN THE SHADOW OF YOUR WINGS.
MY SOUL CLINGS TO YOU; YOUR
RIGHT HAND UPHOLDS ME.

—PSALM 63:7-8

As you give yourself more and more to a *life* of constant *communion* with Me, you will find that you simply have no *time* for *worry*.

"Who of you by worrying can add a single hour to his life? Since you cannot do this very little thing, why do you worry about the rest?"

—Luke 12:25–26

ENTRUST YOUR LOVED ONES
TO ME. RELEASE THEM INTO MY
PROTECTIVE CARE. THEY ARE
MUCH SAFER WITH ME THAN IN
YOUR CLINGING HANDS.

The LORD replied,
"My Presence will go with you,
and I will give you *rest*."
—EXODUS 33:14

Waiting, trusting, and hoping are intricately connected: like golden strands interwoven to form a strong chain. Trusting is the central strand, because it is the response from My children that I desire the most.

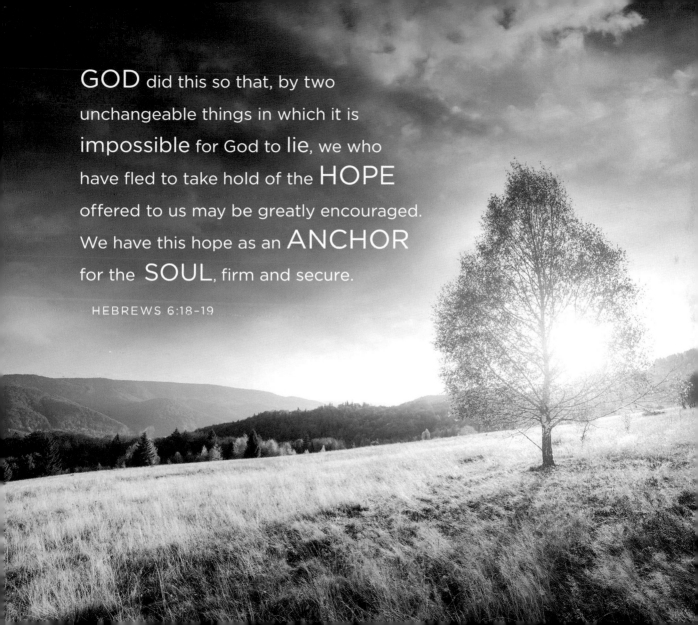

GOD did this so that, by two unchangeable things in which it is impossible for God to lie, we who have fled to take hold of the HOPE offered to us may be greatly encouraged. We have this hope as an ANCHOR for the SOUL, firm and secure.

HEBREWS 6:18–19

I KNOW THE DEPTH AND BREADTH OF YOUR NEED FOR ME.

I CAN READ THE EMPTINESS OF YOUR THOUGHTS WHEN

THEY WANDER AWAY FROM ME.

Be *still* before the LORD
and *wait* patiently for him.

—PSALM 37:7

AS THE HOLY SPIRIT
CONTROLS YOUR MIND
AND ACTIONS MORE FULLY,
YOU BECOME FREE IN ME.
YOU ARE INCREASINGLY
RELEASED TO BECOME THE
ONE I CREATED YOU TO BE.

FOR IT IS GOD WHO WORKS IN YOU
TO WILL AND TO ACT ACCORDING
TO HIS GOOD PURPOSE.

—*Philippians 2:13*

I am ever so near you, hovering over your shoulder, reading every thought. People think that thoughts are fleeting and worthless, but yours are precious to Me.

◇◇◇◇◇◇◇◇◇◇◇◇◇◇◇◇

O Lord, you have searched me and you know me.
You know when I sit and when I rise;
you perceive my thoughts from afar.

—*Psalm 139:1–2*

I have prepared this *day* with the most tender *concern* and attention to detail. Instead of approaching the day as a *blank page* you need to fill up, try *living* it in a responsive mode: being on the *lookout* for all that I am doing.

As for God, his way is perfect; the word of the Lord is flawless. He is a shield for all who take refuge in him.

–PSALM 18:30

Why are you in despair, O my soul?
And why have you become disturbed within me?
Hope in God, for I shall again praise
Him for the help of His presence.

—PSALM 42:5 NASB

Trouble and *distress* are *woven* into the very fabric of this perishing world. Only My Life in you can *empower* you to face this endless flow of problems with *good* cheer.

ANXIETY WRAPS YOU UP IN YOURSELF, TRAPPING YOU IN YOUR OWN THOUGHTS. WHEN YOU LOOK TO ME AND WHISPER MY NAME, YOU BREAK FREE AND RECEIVE MY HELP.

I have strength for all things in Christ Who empowers me [I am ready for anything and equal to anything through Him Who infuses inner strength into me].

—Philippians 4:13 AMP

As you come to Me and take My yoke upon you, I fill you with My very Life. This is how I choose to live in the world and accomplish My purposes. This is also how I bless you with Joy unspeakable and full of Glory.

"Come to me, all you who are weary and burdened, and I will give you rest. Take my yoke upon you and learn from me, for I am gentle and humble in heart, and you will find rest for your souls."

—Matthew 11:28-29

MY PEACE IS SUCH AN
ALL-ENCOMPASSING GIFT THAT IT IS
INDEPENDENT OF ALL CIRCUMSTANCES.
THOUGH YOU LOSE EVERYTHING ELSE,
IF YOU GAIN MY PEACE YOU ARE
RICH INDEED.

You will keep in perfect peace him whose mind is steadfast,
because he trusts in you.

—ISAIAH 26:3

Let Me be your *positive* focus.

When you look to Me, knowing Me as

God with you, you experience *Joy.*

Delight yourself in the LORD
and he will give you
the desires of your heart.
—*Psalm 37:4*

I love you regardless of how
well you are performing.
Bring your performance anxiety
to Me, and receive in its place
My unfailing Love.

The LORD appeared to us in the past, saying: "I have loved you
with an everlasting love; I have drawn you with loving-kindness."

—JEREMIAH 31:3

When you are weary and everything seems to be going wrong, you can still utter these four words: *"I trust You, Jesus."* By doing so, you release matters into My control, and you fall back into the security of My everlasting arms.

"YOU WILL SEEK ME AND FIND ME WHEN YOU SEEK ME WITH ALL YOUR HEART."

—JEREMIAH 29:13

I hate it when My children grumble, casually despising My sovereignty. Thankfulness is a safeguard against this deadly sin. Furthermore, a grateful attitude becomes a grid through which you perceive life.

Therefore, since we are receiving a kingdom that cannot be shaken, let us be thankful, and so worship God acceptably with reverence and awe.

—Hebrews 12:28–29

Bearing your circumstances bravely—even thanking Me for them—is one of the highest forms of praise. This sacrifice of thanksgiving rings golden-toned bells of Joy throughout heavenly realms. On earth, also, your patient suffering sends out ripples of good tidings in ever-widening circles.

In him our hearts *rejoice,* for we *trust* in his holy name.

—*Psalm 33:21*

PAUSE BEFORE RESPONDING TO PEOPLE OR SITUATIONS, GIVING MY SPIRIT SPACE TO ACT THROUGH YOU.

Do you not know that your body is a temple of the Holy Spirit, who is in you, whom you have received from God? You are not your own.

—1 CORINTHIANS 6:19

I am everywhere at every time, ceaselessly working on your behalf. That is why your best coping strategies are trusting Me and living close to Me.

"DO NOT FEAR, FOR I AM WITH YOU; DO NOT ANXIOUSLY LOOK ABOUT YOU, FOR I AM YOUR GOD. I WILL STRENGTHEN YOU, SURELY I WILL HELP YOU, SURELY I WILL UPHOLD YOU WITH MY RIGHTEOUS RIGHT HAND."

—Isaiah 41:10 NASB

YOUR AWARENESS OF YOUR CONSTANT NEED FOR ME IS YOUR GREATEST STRENGTH. YOUR NEEDINESS, PROPERLY HANDLED, IS A LINK TO MY PRESENCE.

IN THE DAY OF MY TROUBLE I WILL CALL TO YOU,
FOR YOU WILL ANSWER ME.

—Psalm 86:7

In union with Me you are *complete*.

In *closeness* to Me, you are

transformed more and more

into the one I designed you to be.

Now the Lord is the Spirit, and where the Spirit of the Lord is, there is freedom. And we, who with unveiled faces all reflect the Lord's glory, are being transformed into his likeness with ever-increasing glory.

—2 Corinthians 3:17–18

When you spend time with Me,
I restore your sense of direction.
I enable you to do less but
accomplish more.

COMMIT TO THE LORD WHATEVER YOU DO,
AND YOUR PLANS WILL SUCCEED.

—PROVERBS 16:3

SEEK TO PLEASE ME ABOVE ALL ELSE. LET THAT GOAL BE YOUR FOCAL POINT AS YOU GO THROUGH THIS DAY.

"But seek first his kingdom and his righteousness, and all these things will be given to you as well."

—*Matthew 6:33*

I AM NEARER THAN YOU DARE BELIEVE, CLOSER THAN THE AIR YOU BREATHE. IF MY CHILDREN COULD ONLY RECOGNIZE MY PRESENCE, THEY WOULD NEVER FEEL LONELY AGAIN.

GOD MADE HIM WHO HAD NO SIN TO BE SIN
FOR US, SO THAT IN HIM WE MIGHT BECOME
THE RIGHTEOUSNESS OF GOD.

—*2 Corinthians 5:21*

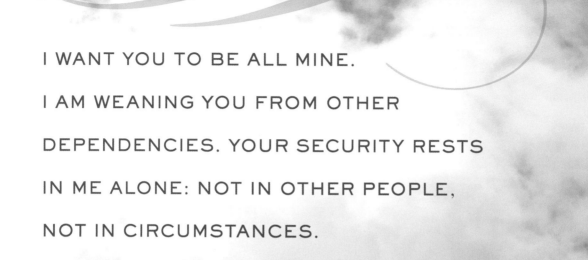

I WANT YOU TO BE ALL MINE.
I AM WEANING YOU FROM OTHER
DEPENDENCIES. YOUR SECURITY RESTS
IN ME ALONE: NOT IN OTHER PEOPLE,
NOT IN CIRCUMSTANCES.

In his heart a man *plans* his course, but the Lord *determines* his steps.

—Proverbs 16:9

The Spirit and the bride say, "Come!" And let him who hears say, "Come!" Whoever is thirsty, let him come; and whoever wishes, let him take the free gift of the water of life.

— *Revelation 22:17*

Come to Me.
Come to Me.
Come to Me.

This is My continual invitation to you,
proclaimed in holy whispers.

OPENNESS TO MY PRESENCE GIVES YOU GLIMPSES OF HEAVEN WHILE YOU STILL RESIDE ON EARTH.

Blessed are those who have learned to acclaim you,
who walk in the light of your presence, O LORD.

—Psalm 89:15

Trust Me in the midst of a messy day.

Your inner calm—your *Peace* in

My *Presence*—need not be shaken

by what is going on around you.

"Peace I leave with you; my peace I give you.

I do not give to you as the world gives.

Do not let your hearts be troubled and do not be afraid."

—*John 14:27*

BE WILLING TO GO OUT ON A *limb* WITH ME. IF THAT IS WHERE I AM *leading* YOU, IT IS THE *safest* PLACE TO BE.

Those who know your name will trust in you, for you, LORD, have never forsaken those who seek you.

—Psalm 9:10

*A thankful attitude
opens windows of heaven.
Spiritual blessings fall freely
onto you through those
openings into eternity.*

PRAISE BE TO THE GOD AND FATHER OF OUR LORD JESUS CHRIST,
WHO HAS BLESSED US IN THE HEAVENLY REALMS
WITH EVERY SPIRITUAL BLESSING IN CHRIST.

—Ephesians 1:3

You are my lamp, O LORD;
the LORD turns my darkness into light.

—2 Samuel 22:29

When you *seek* Me
instead of the world's idols,
you experience My Joy
and Peace.

MY LIGHT SHINES MOST BRIGHTLY THROUGH BELIEVERS WHO TRUST ME IN THE DARK. THAT KIND OF TRUST IS SUPERNATURAL: A PRODUCTION OF MY INDWELLING SPIRIT.

Even in darkness light dawns for the upright, for the gracious and compassionate and righteous man.... He will have no fear of bad news; his heart is steadfast, trusting in the LORD.

—*Psalm 112:4, 7*

The ultimate protection against sinking during life's storms is devoting time to develop your friendship with Me.

The LORD is good to those whose hope is in him,
to the one who seeks him;
it is good to wait quietly for the salvation of the LORD.

—Lamentations 3:25–26

REMEMBER THAT YOUR RELATIONSHIP WITH ME IS SATURATED IN GRACE. THEREFORE, NOTHING YOU DO OR DON'T DO CAN SEPARATE YOU FROM MY PRESENCE.

For it is by grace you have been saved, through faith—and this is not from yourselves, it is the gift of God.

—EPHESIANS 2:8

GLORIFYING AND ENJOYING ME
IS A HIGHER PRIORITY THAN
MAINTAINING A TIDY, STRUCTURED
LIFE. GIVE UP YOUR STRIVING
TO KEEP EVERYTHING UNDER
CONTROL—AN IMPOSSIBLE TASK
AND A WASTE OF PRECIOUS ENERGY.

BUT LET ALL WHO TAKE REFUGE IN YOU BE GLAD; LET THEM EVER SING FOR JOY.
SPREAD YOUR PROTECTION OVER THEM,
THAT THOSE WHO LOVE YOUR NAME MAY REJOICE IN YOU.

—Psalm 5:11

Make Me your focal point *as you move through this day. Just as a spinning ballerina must keep returning her eyes to a given point, to maintain her balance, so you must keep returning your focus to* Me.

This then is how we know that we belong to the truth,
and how we set our hearts at rest in his presence
whenever our hearts condemn us. For God is greater
than our hearts, and he knows everything.

—1 John 3:19–20

MY DEEP DESIRE IS THAT YOU LEARN TO
DEPEND ON ME IN EVERY SITUATION. I MOVE
HEAVEN AND EARTH TO ACCOMPLISH THIS
PURPOSE, BUT YOU MUST COLLABORATE
WITH ME IN THIS TRAINING.

Finally, be *strong* in the Lord
and in his *mighty* power.

—EPHESIANS 6:10

QUIET YOUR MIND
in MY PRESENCE.
THEN YOU WILL BE ABLE
TO HEAR ME BESTOWING
the RESURRECTION BLESSING:
"PEACE BE *with* YOU."

"And surely I am with you always, to the very end of the age."

—Matthew 28:20

*If you try to carry
tomorrow's trouble today,
you will stagger under the load
and eventually fall flat. You must
discipline yourself to live within
the boundaries of today.*

But encourage one another daily, as long as it is
called Today, so that none of you may be
hardened by sin's deceitfulness.

—*Hebrews 3:13*

A LIFE LIVED CLOSE TO ME WILL NEVER BE DULL OR PREDICTABLE. EXPECT EACH DAY TO CONTAIN *surprises!*

This is the day the LORD has made; we will *rejoice* and be glad in it.

—*Psalm 118:24 NKJV*

TASTE AND SEE THAT I AM
GOOD. THE MORE INTIMATELY
YOU EXPERIENCE ME, THE
MORE CONVINCED YOU
BECOME OF MY GOODNESS.

TASTE AND SEE THAT THE LORD IS GOOD;
BLESSED IS THE MAN WHO TAKES REFUGE IN HIM.

—*Psalm 34:8*

Trust IS LIKE A STAFF YOU CAN LEAN ON AS YOU JOURNEY UPHILL WITH ME. IF YOU TRUST IN ME CONSISTENTLY, THE STAFF WILL BEAR AS MUCH OF YOUR WEIGHT AS NEEDED.

Lean on, *trust* in, and be confident in the Lord with all your heart and mind and do not rely on your own insight or understanding.

—Proverbs 3:5 AMP

THE PEACE I GIVE YOU
TRANSCENDS YOUR
INTELLECT. WHEN MOST
OF YOUR MENTAL ENERGY
GOES INTO EFFORTS TO
FIGURE THINGS OUT, YOU
ARE UNABLE TO RECEIVE
THIS GLORIOUS GIFT.

Now may the Lord of peace himself give you peace
at all times and in every way. The Lord be with all of you.

–2 Thessalonians 3:16

Do not let any set of
circumstances intimidate you.
The more challenging your day,
the more of My Power
I place at your disposal.

Look to the LORD and his strength;
seek his face always.

—PSALM 105:4

The more aware you are of My Presence, the safer you feel. This is not some sort of escape from reality; it is tuning in to ultimate reality.

Satisfy us in the morning with your unfailing love, that we may sing for joy and be glad all our days.

—Psalm 90:14

Talk with Me about everything,
letting the Light of My Presence *shine* on
your hopes and plans.

For with you is the *fountain* of *life*;
in your light we see light.
—*Psalm 36:9*

COME TO ME WHEN YOU ARE HURTING, AND I WILL SHARE YOUR PAIN. COME TO ME WHEN YOU ARE JOYFUL, AND I WILL SHARE YOUR JOY— MULTIPLYING IT MANY TIMES OVER.

Shout for joy, O heavens; rejoice, O earth; burst into song, O mountains! For the LORD comforts his people and will have compassion on his afflicted ones.

—ISAIAH 49:13

Remember that you live in a **fallen** world: an abnormal world tainted by sin. Much frustration and failure result from your seeking **perfection** in this life.

~~~~~~~~

Delight yourself in the Lord
and he will give you the desires of your heart.
—Psalm 37:4

Because you are human,

you will always have *ups* and

downs in your life experience.

But the promise of My Presence limits

how far down you can go.

The LORD your God is with you, he is mighty to save.
He will take great delight in you, he will quiet you with his love,
he will rejoice over you with singing.

—*Zephaniah 3:17*

THE SECRET OF BEING
THANKFUL IS LEARNING TO
SEE EVERYTHING FROM MY
PERSPECTIVE. MY WORLD IS
YOUR CLASSROOM. MY WORD
IS A LAMP TO YOUR FEET AND
A LIGHT FOR YOUR PATH.

The heavens declare the glory of God;
and the firmament shows His handiwork.

—PSALM 19:1 NKJV

LIMITATIONS CAN BE LIBERATING, WHEN YOUR STRONGEST DESIRE IS LIVING CLOSE TO ME.

"Be still before the LORD, all mankind, because he has roused himself from his holy dwelling."

—ZECHARIAH 2:13

Marvel at the beauty of a life intertwined with My Presence. Rejoice as we journey together in intimate communion. Enjoy the adventure of finding yourself through losing yourself in Me.

Therefore, if anyone is in Christ, he is a new creation; the old has gone, the new has come!

—2 Corinthians 5:17

THE TRUE QUESTION IS NOT
WHETHER YOU CAN COPE
WITH WHATEVER HAPPENS BUT
WHETHER YOU AND I TOGETHER
CAN HANDLE ANYTHING THAT
OCCURS. IT IS THIS YOU-AND-I-
TOGETHER FACTOR THAT GIVES
YOU CONFIDENCE TO FACE THE
DAY CHEERFULLY.

O God, you are my God, earnestly I seek you.

—PSALM 63:1

I guarantee you will always have problems in your life, but they must not become your focus. When you feel yourself sinking in the sea of circumstances, cry out: "Help me, Jesus!" and I will draw you back to Me.

A BRUISED REED HE WILL NOT BREAK, AND A SMOLDERING WICK HE WILL NOT SNUFF OUT. IN FAITHFULNESS HE WILL BRING FORTH JUSTICE.

—*Isaiah 42:3*

I HAVE DESIGNED YOU TO NEED ME MOMENT BY MOMENT. AS YOUR AWARENESS OF YOUR NEEDINESS INCREASES, SO DOES YOUR REALIZATION OF MY ABUNDANT SUFFICIENCY.

Let us then approach the throne of grace with confidence, so that we may receive mercy and find grace to help us in our time of need.

—*Hebrews 4:16*

Bring Me the sacrifice
of thanksgiving.
Take nothing for granted,
not even the rising of the sun.

I will offer to You the sacrifice of thanksgiving,
and will call upon the name of the LORD.

—*Psalm 116:17 NKJV*

Many are the plans in a man's heart,
but it is the LORD's purpose that prevails.

–Proverbs 19:21

Walk with
Me in holy trust,
responding to
My initiatives rather
than trying to
make things fit
your plans.

Come to Me with a **teachable** spirit,

eager to be changed.

A close walk with Me is a life of continual newness.

You have said, *"Seek my face."*

My heart says to you,

"Your face, LORD, do I seek."

—Psalm 27:8 ESV

DO NOT FEAR MY WILL,
FOR THROUGH IT I ACCOMPLISH
WHAT IS BEST FOR YOU.
TAKE A DEEP BREATH,
AND DIVE INTO THE DEPTHS
OF ABSOLUTE TRUST IN ME.

In the morning, O LORD, you hear my voice;
in the morning I lay my requests before
you and wait in expectation.

–Psalm 5:3

While you wait in **My Presence**, I do My best work within you, transforming you by the renewing of your **mind**.

Do not conform any longer to the pattern of this world, but be transformed by the renewing of your mind.

—*Romans 12:2*

When you walk through a day with childlike

delight, savoring every *blessing*,

you proclaim your *trust* in Me:

your ever-present Shepherd.

But let all who take refuge in you be glad;
let them ever sing for joy.

—*Psalm 5:11*

HUMAN WEAKNESS, CONSECRATED TO ME, *is like a* MAGNET— DRAWING MY POWER *into your* WEAKNESS.

"The LORD, the LORD, is my strength and my song; he has become my salvation." With joy you will draw water from the wells of salvation.

—Isaiah 12:2–3

I have *awakened* in your *heart* a strong

desire to know Me. This longing originated in Me,

though it now *burns* brightly in you.

Finally, brothers, whatever is true, whatever is noble, whatever is right, whatever is pure, whatever is lovely, whatever is admirable—if anything is excellent or praiseworthy—think about such things.

—Philippians 4:8

ANXIOUS THOUGHTS MEANDER

ABOUT AND CRISSCROSS IN YOUR BRAIN,

BUT *trusting* ME BRINGS YOU

DIRECTLY INTO MY PRESENCE.

~~~~~

"Therefore do not worry about tomorrow,
for tomorrow will worry about itself.
Each day has enough trouble of its own."

—*Matthew 6:34*

Listen to Me even while
you are listening to other people.
As they open their souls to your
scrutiny, you are on holy ground.
You need the help of My Spirit to
respond appropriately.

"WHOEVER BELIEVES IN ME, AS THE SCRIPTURE HAS SAID, STREAMS OF LIVING WATER WILL FLOW FROM WITHIN HIM."

—JOHN 7:38

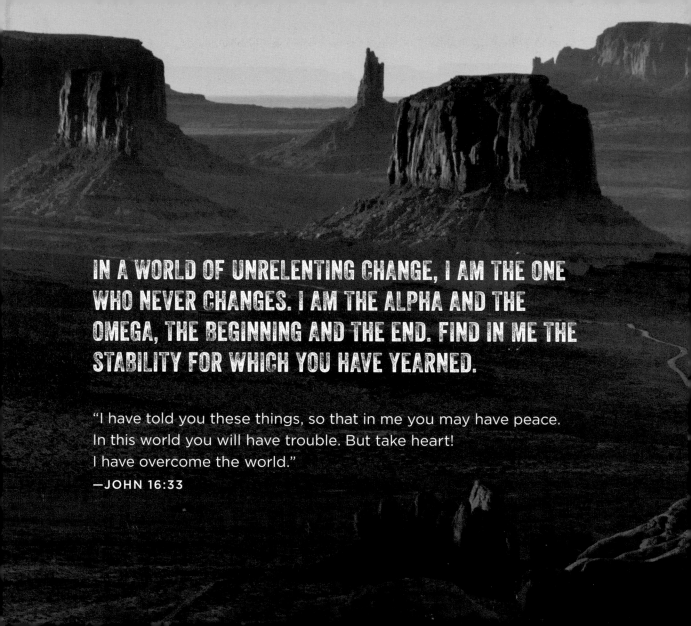

IN A WORLD OF UNRELENTING CHANGE, I AM THE ONE WHO NEVER CHANGES. I AM THE ALPHA AND THE OMEGA, THE BEGINNING AND THE END. FIND IN ME THE STABILITY FOR WHICH YOU HAVE YEARNED.

"I have told you these things, so that in me you may have peace. In this world you will have trouble. But take heart! I have overcome the world."
—JOHN 16:33

"I am making everything new."
—Revelation 21:5